What She Was Wearing

Shawn Aveningo Sanders

A Publication of The Poetry Box®

Book Design by Shawn Aveningo Sanders.
Cover Design by Robert R. Sanders.

These poems are based on a true event. Some of the names
have been changed to protect the innocent.

ISBN: 978-1-948461-32-0
Printed in the United States of America.

Published by The Poetry Box®, 2019
Beaverton, Oregon
ThePoetryBox.com

To those who have suffered in silence

*How long
can you
keep a secret
before
you're completely
unraveled?*

Contents

Another Page in the Fraternity Scrapbook 7

Animal House 8

What I Was Wearing 10

To Call or Not Call the Police 11

(un)Friendly Fire 12

Dial Tone 13

How to Survive Suicide 14

Saving Maggie 15

I Am *What She Was Wearing* 16

Apology 17

I Make a List 19

The Day I Saw My Rapist at the Corner Texaco 20

What Happens Later—Sometimes, Much Later 21

The Four Horsemen of My Apocalypse 23

Prepping My Kids for College 25

A Toga She Wore 26

We Are the B.M.O.C. 27

Binders Full of Women 29

Homecoming Through the Eyes of Brad 30

The Victim Speaks Up 31

Can't Hide the Truth 32

Erasing the Pent-Up Poison 33

You Know This Woman 35

Unfurling 36

There Will Be Days 37

Acknowledgments 41

What They're Saying ... 43

About the Author 47

About The Poetry Box 48

Another Page in the Fraternity Scrapbook

Flash … Pop … Flash!

A familiar sound—
yet, not one I was expecting
in my groggy, drugged,
slurred-word state.

Flash … Pop … Again!

This time he pauses,
reaches for another
flash-cube from his shirt
pocket.

Flash … Frantic … Scream!

I lunge   for the Kodak.
I rip out the film.
He rips out another
handful of my hair.

Flash … Pop … Swish!

Glint of sheen,
a knife, I scream
again … louder … *Please Help!*

Animal House

I wake to a nightmare.
Vision blurred by camera flash.
My cries
merely beckon more monsters
in men's clothing.

My wrists and ankles
bound by their rage,
I'm trapped
like a mouse
foolishly believing in cheese.

I look deep into their shark-dead eyes.
Tears flood mine.

Please stop.
Oh merciful Lord
I beg you—
make them stop.
Another prayer—
unanswered.

He's done.
He's won.
Now's my chance
to run,
before another
takes his plunge.
I escape,

bury myself in a blanket—
alone here with my shame,
not enough pills to numb the pain.

Thirty years later,
I remember
(but can barely
utter) his name.

What I Was Wearing

Pink sheet twisted into a toga
over a white one-piece swimsuit,
pink chiffon bow in my hair,
Nana's rhinestone dangly earrings,
pink lace fingerless gloves, silver
glittery sandals, a spritz of *Georgio*,
frosted mulberry lipstick,
and a big smile.

This is what I wore to the party.

And then I woke up to a strap
falling off one shoulder,
the other strap cut
revealing my breast,
a drop of blood
where the knife
nicked my flesh, the crotch
of my swimsuit sliced in half,
spilled beer, stained sheet,
the scent of cheap cologne,
four sets of fingerprints—

This is what I wore running home.

To Call or Not Call the Police

That
is a monumental
decision
for this young woman
whose lips have kissed
bottles of Boone's Farm
and Budweiser
ever clear
of the laws she has
broken
partying and partaking
before reaching legal age
on *this* side
of the state line

In the heartland
where girls are taught
to play hard-to-get
and *boys will be boys*
how could she prove
to the good-ole-boys in blue
that she's not the one to blame
she's not a slut
and she definitely
did not
ask for it

(un)Friendly-Fire

A soldier, mistakenly shot down by
his own troops, is known as a victim
of friendly-fire.

When the touch is
uninvited.

When the slumber is
unexpected.

When she wakes
undressed.

When the attacker is
unknown—

or worse . . .

Dial Tone

Payphone
down the hall.
No privacy.

Must wait
for the right
moment.

It's quiet
and dark.
Call now.

Fingers tremble,
hovering
atop silver buttons.

Just three numbers.
Come on—
You can do this.

9 . . . . . .
. . . 1 . . .
. 1

911 What's your emergency?
Hello?
Click.

Dial tone—
I whisper
please   help   me

How to Survive Suicide

Don't leave a note.
Your final plea for help
may bring unwanted advice.

Make a mixed tape
(translation: playlist).
Let your favorite songs be your final lullaby.

Be frugal.
Buy the generic sleeping pills.
Believe the "compare to" claims on the label.

Speaking of labels,
ignore the dosing instructions. Indulge.
Gluttony's a mere second-rate sin.

Wash the pills down
with a *Yoohoo.*
No need to count calories now.

Double-check the deadbolt.
Laugh at the irony
of that particular oxymoron.

Turn out the lights.
Snuggle under grandmother's quilt.
Whisper apologies until you're fast asleep.

Wake-up
thirty-five hours later and wonder
if anyone noticed you were gone.

Saving Maggie

I survived the rape and the failed suicide. Haunted by my secret, I tried to act normal. Finals were approaching, so my sorority sisters and I turned the lounge into a study hall. We prepped for exams & shared notes. But mostly, we gabbed about the upcoming sorority spring formal— hoping the boys we liked would accept our invitation.

Maggie burst into the room. She had big news! Brad had just agreed to be her date for the Alpha Xi dance. After all the commotion:

> *Oh my God, he's sooooo dreamy.*

> > *What are you going to wear?*

> *I can do your hair & make-up.*

> > *Do you think he'll pick you up in a limo?*

I whispered in Maggie's ear, *Can we talk?*

Maggie was a sweet, shy girl who didn't date often. She was a straight-A student, lettered in softball, and was the kind of girl who would go out of her way to help a friend in need—no matter what. I had to step up. I had to warn her.

Maggie didn't go to that dance with Brad. She didn't go to the dance with anyone. It would have been fun helping her pick out a dress. (Her favorite color was peach.) But, at least, no one ever asked her, afterward

> > *what she was wearing.*

I Am *What She Was Wearing*

I don't understand all the fuss.
Measure for measure, I'm merely
a wide bolt of cotton fabric. Nothing
fancy, except for that thin row of lace
adorning my top edge.
      She had to do
all the work—twisting, contorting me
into something wearable.
       As I compare
myself to the other togas, I have to say,
Damn I look fine.
      What?
You don't think a sheet has body-
shaming issues or feelings of envy?
We *all* do. There's no escaping it.
       You
keep up with the Joneses while we gossip
over thread counts & wrinkles.
       Sorry,
I digress—must be from a lack of sleep.
She kept me out late last night, way past
my bedtime.
      Did something bad happen?
My memory is a bit foggy. This morning,
I found myself crumpled in the corner—
smelling of beer and sloe gin
wrinkled and wet and torn and
        dirty.
I suppose now
I'll be the one blamed.

Apology

I'm not sure what feels worse
       afterwards
the shame   or the guilt?

I now know
      it wasn't my fault.
(That's not what I'm talking about here.)

What about the other girls?
The girls who came
        after me.

How many more girls
    trusted him?
    let him open the car door?
    drank the Budweiser he poured?

How many more screams were silenced?

How many more girls
    tried to escape?
    ran home in the dark?

How many more
    tried to end it all with pills?
            a razor blade?
            a bed sheet?
            a coat hanger?
            a gun?

How many more . . .
How many more girls could I have saved?

Dear sisters:
    Please accept my apology.
    I was so fucking afraid

                        to speak up
            that I let all of you

                        down.

I Make a List

I trace each step
trying to remember
exactly
how it all happened,
trying to account
for each mistake
I may have made.

Was it my own damn fault?
What could I have done
differently
to prevent it
from ever happening
to me
or anyone else?

I make a list
and only find a few mistakes
in the end—

I went away to college.
I joined a sorority.
I celebrated *Greek Week*.
I wore a toga.
I applied lipstick.
I tied a bow in my hair.
I wanted to look pretty.
I danced.
I enjoyed myself.
I had a few drinks.
I believed he liked me.
I did not report the rape.
I did not trust in my friends for help.
I kept my secret bottled inside for years.

The Day I Saw My Rapist at the Corner Texaco

I remember holding the fuel nozzle in my hand,
staring at him for what seemed an eternity.

I was bisected—
    half of me desperate
    to spray gasoline across the concrete divide
    and light a match,

while the other half
    wanted to peel away my skin
    to swap with another human to hide.

My babies—
    all three of them lined up in their car seats
    in the backseat of my Honda.

Two little girls peacefully asleep,
while their brother pointed his chubby finger
    at a ladybug on the windshield
    and laughed.

What Happens Later—
Sometimes, Much Later

One Sunday,
you're watching football on TV—
some team you don't normally pay attention to,
and out of the blue
you hear
that name.

The same name as the one who raped you.
(the one you trusted years ago)
He has one of those all-too-common names
like John Smith, Sam Johnson,
Mike Brown, or Brad Jones.
And yet it's still a name you haven't heard
in more than a decade.

And there it is
again,
rolling off the tongue of the announcer,
that name emblazoned
in bright white letters on a dark purple jersey.
That name—
the new starting quarterback
this team's new hope for glory.

Touchdown!
You hear the name again
blasting now in surround-sound.
You knock over a beer bottle,
drop the 7-layer dip,
spill the football-shaped bowl
of tortilla chips,
and tremble.

While everyone cheers,
you quietly clean up the mess
and hope no one notices,
or bothers to ask:
What's Wrong?

The Four Horsemen
of My Apocalypse

-One-

It was you, the cute shy guy in uniform, who smiled at me almost every day as I walked by on my way to lunch. You never said a word. Then one day, *Hey, you going to the party tonight? Maybe I'll see you there.* My response—A simple smile. Maybe it wasn't the response you expected. Maybe I should have said *YES, absolutely, I'll see you there.* Would that have altered the outcome? Would we had simply shared a dance and a few beers? Would the night had been filled with conversation?—you sharing your fly-boy dreams, me hanging on every word as our hands slide slowly together. But that's not how it went down. You, Brad, had a different plan all along.

-Two-

You were his best friend, Sam. I can't remember ever seeing either one of you at a party without the other close by. His wing man—like in the movies. But this isn't *Pretty in Pink.* Instead, you become his accomplice, co-conspirator, obeying his every command. The perfect partner in crime. Loyal. Obedient. Willing to settle for sloppy seconds.

-Three-

I remember you, Dick. You sat behind me in Calculus. You had always been nice to me. You were his roommate but not his best friend, not his number two. The way I see it you were the weakest link. Shorter than the others and not strong enough to hold me down on your own. You're the one whose grasp I finally escaped. Seeing you in class, a week later, I wanted to ask, *Did you let me go out of mercy?* I'll never know. I dropped the class.

-Four-

Today, that's all he is. The fourth man-boy whose name I cannot remember, or perhaps never really knew. I sometimes wonder was there more, something I've forgotten, perhaps on purpose. Did I compartmentalize, bury it too deep? Does his name evoke a detail so dark, so painful, so ugly-sinister-heartbreaking-fearful-disgusting-shameful, that my conscience cannot allow it back in? I don't know. I may never know. For now, I'll call him Joe.

Prepping My Kids for College

I knew the day would come.
The day I would have to let my secret out,
tell my story.
For ignorance is dangerous,
not bliss.

I'd have to make the hard choice –
remove my children's veil of invincibility.
Make them understand,
rape isn't something that only happens
to *other* people.

• • •

Their heads bowed down like wilting roses.
They reached for my trembling hand.
We held each other. We cried.
I felt my shame
morph into courage.

I didn't teach my daughters
how to *avoid* rape that day.
I didn't buy them a whistle.
Instead, I taught my son
the horrid ugliness of the crime
against a woman, a girl, a mother, a sister...

• • •

When I told their father about our talk,
he asked me if I told them

what I was wearing.

A Toga She Wore

A toga she wore, like never before.
A sheet she bought from the corner store—
pretty-in-pink and trimmed in white lace,
rhinestone earrings that framed her face
—an upgrade from typical togas of yore.

Together they danced and danced some more.
She had no idea what was in store,
when he invited her to his place.
A toga she wore.

A drug in her drink: the one he had poured.
Held down by the others—in all there were four.
If only she had a spray can of mace.
Struggling for freedom, she spat in his face.

Instead of pretty, she felt like a whore.
A toga—it was a toga she wore.

We Are the B.M.O.C.
(Big Men on Campus)

Oh, come on, Baby—
We had fun tonight.

Remember how we danced?
How the DJ played Thriller
and a crowd circled around us.
You knew every dance move.
Applause and cameras flashing—
we were the hit of the party.
Such a thrill!
You didn't seem to mind the camera, then.

So why such a fuss?
Why do you have to scream?
I just wanted to take a few photos,
pose you in half-naked glory,
show the guys how pretty you are.

Everything would have been fine.
But you had to make a scene.
Who do you think you are, ripping out the film like that?

    * * *

Hey Sam,
Can you believe what this bitch did?
I think it's time we teach her a lesson.

Dick, Joe,
You two hold her ankles.
Sam, you take her hands,

wrap her wrists with that necktie
hanging from my bedpost.

She's still pretty groggy.
We can each take a turn.
There's no way she can fight
against the four of us.

    * * *

You see, Doll, these guys are my brothers.
They would do anything for me.
ANYTHING.
Make sure you remember that.

No one   will ever   believe you.

Binders Full of Women

It wasn't until after the attack
I discovered the binder. Forty-seven

girls drugged, stripped, photographed,
raped. Page 48 sat empty, waiting

for the photo they took of me. Greek
Council enforced a crackdown on hazing,

but for this, the fraternity had no such
policy in place. Buried beneath public

philanthropy and brotherhood, lie
bones of broken sisters, shattered souls,

shards of shame — a mosaic whose mortar
weakened year by year, woman by woman

bravely blowing the lid off Pandora's box.

Homecoming Through the Eyes of Brad

His daughter is riding in a float down Main Street.
Her sisterhood embroidered in bright blue & gold
Greek letters across her chest.

He's glad sororities don't haze pledges like his fraternity did.
But he does worry about those secret ceremonies.
How many stories from the past are shared by candlelight?

He hasn't been sleeping very well, lately.
The headlines have been whirling in his head.
Will his past come back to haunt him, too—

> *I can't even remember that girl's name.*
> *She probably doesn't remember mine either.*
> *I don't believe she ever reported the incident.*
>
> *Did she tell anyone in her sorority?*
> *—now my daughter's new sorority.*
> *Did she ever tell anyone at all?*
>
> *Maybe I'll call Sam, Dick, and Joe.*
> *Reminisce over a few brewski's.*
> *Make sure we have our story straight.*
> *Just in case.*

The Victim Speaks Up

(Or How I Imagine a Trial,
Had I the Courage Back Then)

I realize the risk:
I may be held in contempt,
cuffed, locked away—
I'm already quite familiar
how restraint feels
against my will.

My question,
Your Honor, you in the black robe
perched high upon your bench:
Do *you* know how it feels?

Do you know
the taste of betrayal
      { bitter   iron   rust }
from a man you labeled friend?

How his fingers tightening around your wrist
      { nails   piercing   flesh }
felt more frightening, more rigid
than cold steel cuffs ever could.

Or how sound slips away—
your own voice stifled
as *he* calls for help
to hold   you   down.

Can't Hide the Truth*

Spring, 1994

~~Sam,~~

~~Son of a bitch number two. I don't know who's worse:
you or Brad.~~ **I** ~~guess you're both equally despicable. You~~
know~~, when I was screaming for help, I actually believed
that you were coming to my rescue. But no, you frat boys
really know how to stick together.~~ **What** ~~a bunch of crap.
I can't believe out of that whole fraternity house not one of~~
you ~~had enough balls to help me. None of you even cared.~~
All ~~you cared about was having another conquest for the
scrapbook. So, tell me, what does it feel like to help someone
rape a helpless girl?~~ **Did** ~~you feel really strong? Did you feel
like a man? Well, you're not! You probably never will be. Poor
you. You didn't even really get your turn. But I'm sure you told
all your buddies you were in on the action. I hope you rot in
Hell!!!~~

*Almost ten years after the rape, a therapist advised me to write letters to my attackers
in order to vent my anger. Now another 25 years later, I find two of the letters and
create these erasure poems. The healing has finally begun.

Erasing the Pent-up Poison*

Spring, 1994

~~Brad,~~

~~You son of a bitch!!!!!! Just who in the hell do you think you are? I can't believe~~ **I was stupid** ~~enough to go back to your dorm room with you.~~ **And** ~~to think I always~~ **thought** ~~you were such a gentleman. Always so polite opening the door for me on our way into accounting class and looking so sharp in your uniform. What a disgrace to the Air Force you turned out to be. You're so sick!!!!! I'll never forget how shocked I was to awaken on the couch to you pulling my toga off and trying to take my picture. And you even seemed appalled at me when I ripped the film out and slammed your camera into the sink, as if I had been the crazy one. Well guess what, I'm not the psycho here. YOU ARE. I HATE YOU !!!!!! I should have turned your ass into the police so you could rot in prison and~~ **everyone** ~~would have known just how horrible you really are. But you got lucky.~~ **I** **was** ~~too scared. I was too ashamed and didn't want anyone on campus to find out. After all it would have ended up being the whole fraternity~~ **against me. But** ~~I guess you were counting on that~~ **now** ~~weren't you. You're so weak. Do you honestly think~~

~~you could have raped me without the help of your buddies,
like Sam. No, I don't think so. I would have been able~~ **to
free myself** ~~and I would have poked your eyes out
so you could never see again and then permanently mutilate
your penis so that you would be in pain for the rest~~ **of** ~~your
life. I wish I could have had~~ **the** ~~courage to lock you up so
that you couldn't have~~ **hurt** ~~anyone else. Do you remember
Maggie who asked you to our sorority spring formal? You
really liked her, didn't you? Well, I'm the reason she stopped
dating you. I'm the reason she cancelled her invitation for you
to take her to formal. That's right, I told her about your little
photography project. Thank God I was at least able to help
one girl. But I believe everybody gets what they have coming
to them.~~ **And** ~~you will probably pay very dearly (if you
haven't already) for~~ **the pain** ~~you have caused me and
anybody else you have hurt. I hope you die a very long and
painful death.~~ **I** ~~hope you grow old alone and never~~ **have**
~~anyone~~ **to** ~~love you. You are nothing!!! God may~~ **forgive**
~~you but I never will.~~

You Know This Woman

As the victims speak out
As the accused are punished
As courage is discovered
And the stories multiply

Perhaps
You're wondering
When?   Where?   Who?

Yes.
You've met her.
You know this woman.
Gaze upon her with kind eyes.

She's ready to rise.

Unfurling

I want to
unfold.
I want to release
these creases
in my earthly, abundant flesh.
Not to smooth
out
nor over,
not to
remove.
But to bear witness to my own secrets
buried deep within,
to find a new truth—
perhaps one disguised as forgetfulness.

I want to hold a flame—
minus the candle,
minus the wick.
Let this light in my palm
show me the shadows,
reveal my scars.

I want to feel the intensity,
immense pain—
that which foretells unbearable joy.
To feel again my own splitting—
the splendor of childbirth,
this time
swaddling my own
self.

I want to unfurl,
pluck each translucent petal—
I love me.   I love me not.   Yes. I love me.

There Will Be Days

A trigger will transport you
where you didn't plan to go—

    Scent of juniper
        wafting from your in-laws' hedge
        while visiting their mountain home.
        You recall gin is made from juniper berries,
            which reminds you of sloe gin,
            and then you remember
                          the smell of his breath.

    The accidental scrape of fingernail
        against a crisp, white-linen tablecloth
        elicits synaptic electricity,
        a snap.
            And suddenly,
            it's *your* fingernails scraping
            a bedsheet, clawing the dark
                        trying to escape.

    Careless Whisper
        plays on the car radio,
        and as much as you love George Michael
        you change the station.
            This song a painful reminder
            of that empty bottle of sleeping pills
            and the belief
                    you're *never gonna dance again.*

But there will be many days
when happiness persists—

    The wonder in your son's eyes
        meeting his twin baby sisters.

How he slips into that big brother role
in an instant,
        picking up a baby bottle
        to help with the feeding,
                and you kiss his tiny blonde head.

The cleverness of two little girls,
        the night they moved a mattress
        into the hallway outside your bedroom,
        perhaps to be closer to you,
        perhaps to prove that they can.
                You trip over the mess
                ready to scold them,
                their giggles so contagious,
                        you can't help but join the laughter.

There will be
        home runs / blue ribbons / birthdays
        family reunions / weddings / graduations
        school plays / prom dresses / soccer games
        old friends / new friends / celebrations
        new jobs / new houses / promotions
        new dreams / new life / new loves

and through it all
        you will re-discover yourself,
        your purpose, your essence,
        your sexuality,
        and finally realize
                how beautiful you are,
                how strong you always have been,
                and how to accept love
                from a man who never once asked

                        what you were wearing.

Acknowledgments

Many thanks to the esteemed publications that first ushered these poems into the world, some in slightly different versions:

"Another Page in the Fraternity Scrapbook" was first published in *American Journal of Poetry* (July, 2018)

"The Day I Saw My Rapist at the Corner Texaco" was first featured in *HEArt (Human Equity through Art) Journal* (Fall, 2015), and reprinted in *Red Sky: poetry on the global epidemic of violence against women* (Sable Books, 2016)

"What Happens Later — Sometimes Much Later" first appeared in *Awakened Voices* (May, 2018)

"Prepping My Kids for College" was first published in *Red Sky: poetry on the global epidemic of violence against women* (Sable Books, 2016)

"Binders Full of Women" first appeared in *VoiceCatcher: a journal of women's voices and visions* (Summer, 2014)

"Unfurling" was featured in *Blue Heron Review* (June 2019, Featured Poet)

∾

I'm not sure I would have had the courage to publish my story had it not been for the bravery of the many women across the world who have shared their stories through the #MeToo movement. Thank you Tarana Burke for igniting that spark, bringing survivors together in solidarity. Who knew a hashtag could be so powerful? Together we are strong!

I'd like to express my gratitude to my dear writing friends, the Feral Poets: Carolyn Martin, Cathy Cain, Tricia Knoll, Pattie Palmer-Baker and Maggie Chula, whose kindness and literary prowess helped me refine many of the poems in this collection.

I'd also like to thank my amazing children: Jimmy, Ashley & Nicole, who showed maturity and compassion beyond their years when I first told them about my experience, as I hoped to better prepare them for a world that is not always kind.

Many heartfelt thanks to my parents, especially my mom, who never judged me, understanding my fear and why it took so long for me to share my story with not only her, but anyone.

And finally, to my wonderful husband, Robert, whose unwavering support, empathy, and love helped me find the strength to release these poems into the world in my quest to help others heal.

Dedicated "to those who have suffered in silence," this book is a testimony to Shawn Aveningo Sanders' courage. For thirty years, she kept a secret that verged on unraveling her, a secret so devastating she once attempted suicide. But here she transcends the traps of shame and self-reproach to confront—in a sequence of poems and epistolary prose—the four men who, as college fraternity brothers, raped her. Forced into silence for too long, women all over this world are now speaking out, saying #MeToo. *What She Was Wearing* is Sanders' brave voice joining this transforming chorus.

—Paulann Petersen, Oregon Poet Laureate Emerita

Shawn Aveningo Sanders' story of living with the aftermath of violence emerges like a geode that's been cracked open after years underground. Each image has been remembered and re-remembered, stored, pressurized, and slowly shaped into a single facet of the experience. From the earrings she was wearing to explaining the assault to her college-age children years later, Aveningo Sanders spares no detail and lets no one off the hook. Starkly honest and memorably graceful, these poems are a virtuoso performance of feminism and survival, as well as a wholly human story that far too many women will understand.

—Amy Miller, author of *The Trouble with New England Girls*

Some of the women and girls who've spoken out in the #MeToo movement have spoken in anguish, and in grief. Some have spoken in shame. In *What She Was Wearing*, Shawn Aveningo Sanders has turned that shame, anguish and grief into poetry, as poets have done for thousands of years. Most of us read about the assaults sustained by those women and girls online, connecting with their words through machines. Here, we learn about their flesh and blood, their spirit, in a profoundly different -- indeed, a classic -- form, in poems. When poems are made of fear and rage, do the readers of those poems feel fear and rage? When art is made of pain, does it hurt its audience? Or does it teach that audience about pain in a way they will absorb and comprehend, creating deep levels of empathy?

The latter effect is surely likely for Shawn Aveningo Sanders' poems, poems that persist in questioning personal responsibility over decades, struggling yet to understand. The variety of form the poet has chosen (compelling in its inclusion of lists, erasures, rhyming stanzas), and the characters she has included (her own children, years later; the girl she saved from the rapist who attacked her) are notable choices, moving readers from personal history, the event itself—still burning inside the body of the poet, to social history in this time of burning revelation.

—Judith Arcana, poet & activist for reproductive rights
author of Announcements from the Planetarium

Instead of pretty, she felt like a whore. A toga—it was a toga she wore. This, from a poem in Shawn Aveningo Sanders' *What She Was Wearing*, feels like a call to every "mythology" of rape: the fraternal sexual assault under the guise of Greek hedonism, the dismissal of damage, and the culture of secrecy and shame. Shawn's work reminds me that riveting poetry sometimes is not so much about the language and the "craft" as it is the bravery and the honesty—the simplicity of reality and rawness of emotion. This bareness is what is fresh and unflinching in Shawn's work. Wearing a toga is not inviting gang rape. Being able to unmask the predators/the past is the voicing of courage. She wears it well.

—Leslie Anne Mcilroy, award-winning poet
co-founder of HEArt, Human Equity through Art

What She Was Wearing begins with the author's violation by men whom she once considered friends. The reader is not permitted to look away as Shawn Aveningo Sanders recounts a terrifying story that is all too familiar, a maddening reminder that rape can happen to anyone, anywhere, without warning. These poems also remind us of the damage caused by blaming the victim. *What She Was Wearing* demonstrates how sexual assault impacts the entirety of the survivor's life and shows us how one can fight their way back to feeling whole again.

Unfortunately, the story Aveningo Sanders shares is one of many. Books like this one ought to be distributed to our daughters and sons so that one day sexual violence will no longer be a commonplace occurrence. May all who have endured such horrors someday find the strength to tell their story as a step on the road to healing and may each person who reads this book benefit from the poet's courage to speak truth to power.

—Christopher Luna
Clark County, WA's inaugural poet laureate (2013-2017)
author of *Message from the Vessel in a Dream*

I'm a little uncertain how to adequately express my admiration, if admiration is the right word to use when the subject is gang rape of an innocent, but Shawn Aveningo Sanders' poetry on this brutal subject stunned me. As a fellow #MeToo survivor, all 25 poems in the book spoke to me, but particularly "Can't Hide the Truth," in such an unusual form; "How to Survive Suicide," for its last lines, *Wake up / thirty-five hours later and wonder/ if anyone noticed you were gone*; as well as the persona poems, but especially the title poem, "I Am What She Was Wearing"—for that last stanza, written from the toga's voice. These poems promise to build a bridge of solidarity for an untold number of women. It's also a must-read for young men.

—Sharon Wood Wortman, poet, storyteller
author of *The Portland Bridge Book*

About the Author

Shawn Aveningo Sanders grew up in St Louis, Missouri and after a bit of globetrotting finally landed in Portland, Oregon, where she miraculously overcame her lifelong fear of birds upon meeting two baby juncos in her backyard. She believes poetry is the perfect literary art form for today's fast-paced world, due to its power to stir emotion in less than two minutes.

Shawn wasn't always a writer. She graduated *Summa cum Laude* and earned a degree in Computer Science with a minor in Marketing from University of Maryland, while working for U.S. Army Logistics in Stuttgart, (West) Germany. Through the years, she's been a software developer, real-estate agent, productivity coach, soccer mom, PTA president, website designer, and book publisher/designer. At various crossroads, her inner-muse would appear, urging Shawn to follow her passion for poetry.

Since 2008, Shawn's work has appeared globally in over 150 literary journals and anthologies. She's a Pushcart nominee (2015), Best of the Net nominee (2017), co-founder of The Poetry Box® press, as well as managing editor for *The Poeming Pigeon*. She was named Best Female Poet-Performer in the *Sacramento News & Review* Reader Poll (2009) and was winner of the first poetry slam in Placerville, California (2012).

Shawn is a proud mother of three amazing adults, and she shares the creative life with her husband, Robert. You can learn more about her at RedShoePoet.com.

About The Poetry Box

The Poetry Box® is a boutique publishing company that enjoys providing a platform for both established and emerging poets to share their words with the world through beautiful printed books and chapbooks.

Feel free to visit the online bookstore (thePoetryBox.com), where you'll find more titles including:

Giving Ground by Lynn M. Knapp

Psyche's Scroll by Karla Linn Merrifield

November Quilt by Penelope Scambly Schott

Shrinking Bones by Judy K. Mosher

Epicurean Ecstasy by Cynthia Gallaher

Surreal Expulsion by D.R. James

The Unknowable Mystery of Other People by Sally Zakariya

Impossible Ledges by Dianne Avey

Bee Dance by Cathy Cain

Like the O in Hope by Jeanne Julian

Call My Name by Heather Wyatt

Shadow Man by Margaret Chula

and more . . .

www.ingramcontent.com/pod-product-compliance
Lightning Source LLC
Chambersburg PA
CBHW051012050726
47592CB00007B/2817